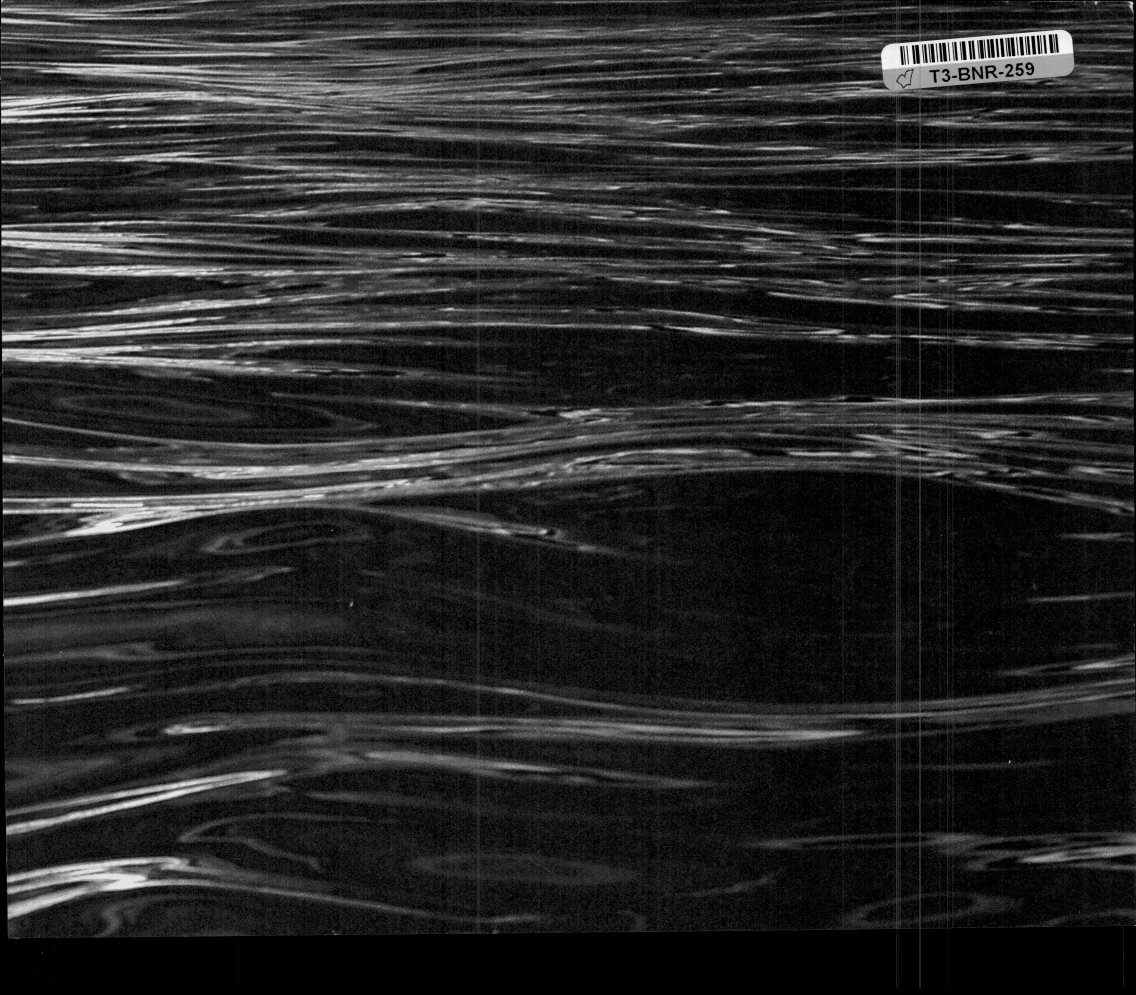

DISCOVERY

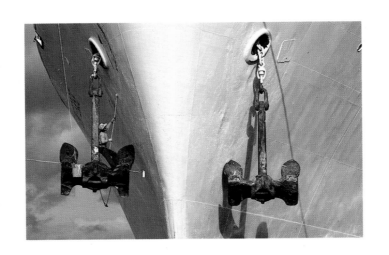

DISCOVERY

The Adventure of Shipboard Education

Text and Photographs by Paul Liebhardt

Foreword by Lloyd Lewan

Edited by Judy Rogers

WILLIAM & ALLEN

The SS *Universe* is registered in Liberia.

Photograph of James Lough on page 14
courtesy New York University Archives.

Published by WILLIAM & ALLEN,
P.O. BOX 6147, Olympia, WA 98502

Library of Congress Catalog Card Number
85-050383
ISBN 0-9614403-0-9

Project Director: Don A. Rogers

Printed in Singapore
First Edition

Dedication

"Ships can transport ideas as well as cargo," C. Y. Tung was fond of saying. College students and educators from around-the-world have discovered he was right. The participants of Semester at Sea, past, present and future, will always be grateful for his unwavering commitment to shipboard education. It is to the memory of C. Y. Tung that this book is dedicated.

To the hundreds of Semester at Sea alumni who
urged that this project be undertaken and to the
one man who insisted on it, Don A. Rogers,
my sincerest thanks. —P. L.

Contents

Foreword   10

The History of Shipboard Education   12

Semester at Sea Today   29

The Departure   31

The Sea   39

The Land   49

The People of the World   63

The SS Universe and Life at Sea   103

The World as a Classroom   121

The Experience   151

The Final Port   171

Afterword   177

Bibliography   179

Foreword

*We must educate people today for a future in which the choices to be faced
cannot be anticipated by even the wisest among us now.*

John Fitzgerald Kennedy

It is a special privilege for me to write the foreword for this extraordinary photographic essay which depicts so well the experience many know as "Semester at Sea." For those who have not had the opportunity to participate in shipboard education, I hope this work will give you a feeling for the warmth, understanding, and personal growth that make this kind of education so special. For those who have experienced a semester at sea, I hope this collection of photographs will keep alive your commitment to international peace and understanding.

Semester at Sea is about the future—your future, the future of your children, and the future of all those who inhabit planet earth. Our world is shrinking; countries have become interdependent. We must strengthen the bonds between peoples and nations. Our success or failure will determine the quality of our collective lives in the years ahead. I believe that either we educate young people for the reality of world interdependence or we mis-educate them; we cannot be neutral.

Semester at Sea is an attempt to address this reality. The program was created to take learners on a self-contained vessel with a select group of scholar/guides on an around-the-world voyage. Students can see for themselves the similarities among peoples and the wonderful differences we know as cultures. Through shipboard courses and guided field experiences, the program provides the framework for a lifetime of learning, concern, and commitment.

Today more than ever, young people must make decisions for themselves, their nations, and their planet with equal attention and concern for all three. No nation today can make any realistic, prudent, or lasting decision without considering the impact on other peoples and nations. Future leaders of all nations must be educated with a long-term view and an understanding of global realities. For the young to use their own lifetimes as bench marks for change is simply not sufficient. The great challenges of the twenty-first century—nuclear weaponry, terrorism, over-population, declining natural resources, hunger, and human rights—cannot be solved in national isolation or in an individual's lifetime. A long-term world view passed from generation to generation must become the beacon for world peace.

The Semester at Sea program contributes to this global view by exposing students to the world's problems, by educating students about world politics, and by openly explaining the ineffectiveness of short-term solutions. Participants come away with the realization that learning is not limited to the classroom, and that learning can be enjoyable. Students become aware that teachers are human beings with much to offer outside the classroom, and that fellow students are often insightful teachers. They discover that reading about a culture, and then experiencing it, creates unparalled learning excitement.

The important aspects of the program for the larger society are the students' increased awareness of global issues, increased tolerance for diversity, and expanded views of their own culture. These new insights make them better students on their home campuses. They tend to create a ripple effect, which heightens awareness of world issues among their families and their student colleagues. Program participants express a commitment to educate their children in a way that will include international involvement.

Keeping shipboard education viable has required dedication and commitment from many sources. There are, however, probably five factors that have most contributed to the survival of shipboard education. First are the alumni, for without them telling others of the merits of Semester at Sea, there would be no program. The quality and quantity of future participants depends almost entirely on the alumni. Second, the leadership of the Institute for Shipboard Education and the university sponsors, especially those who have served on board ship, has been more significant than most realize. Third, the men and women who have served as visiting faculty and staff over the years have been central to the success of each voyage. Fourth, the concept of shipboard education is a sound one, most appropriate to this time and place in our history. It is an excellent example of the whole being greater than the sum of its parts. Fifth, the contribution of the late C. Y. Tung must be considered the major force in maintaining the program over the last decade.

Semester at Sea is an extraordinary educational enterprise. It is the largest undergraduate international program in the world today. Each year more than 800 college students participate in an academic voyage around the world. A nonprofit educational corporation contracts with a major American university, and with one of the largest shipping companies in the world, to produce the Semester at Sea program. When six hundred students, faculty, staff, and crew come together for the first time on the day of departure, they create a fully functioning university.

While traditional study abroad is designed to prepare students for an in-depth experience in a single culture, Semester at Sea provides a unique opportunity to gain an introduction to a minimum of ten cultures from both the developed and developing world. Semester at Sea is an international extension of the traditional undergraduate program. It may also be characterized as a prelude to other international experiences. Most who experience Semester at Sea are motivated to further international study and travel.

The full internationalism of the program is my dream for the future of Semester at Sea. My hope is that one day large numbers of students from several countries will share a ship or many ships for this valuable experience. Shipboard education will have realized its international potential when prominent universities around the world join forces to support experience-based international education. Perhaps one day a fleet of ships sponsored by the United Nations will fulfill this dream. This would be the greatest experiment in cross-cultural living and learning ever undertaken. I believe that such a program could be the loom on which the fabric of world peace is woven.

It has been hard in these few paragraphs to capture the essence of Semester at Sea. Having been involved in shipboard education for eighteen years, I believe in young people more than ever—and especially in their ability to lead us into the twenty-first century. I also firmly believe that Semester at Sea is one of the most important programs in higher education today, providing the basis for a greater understanding of the complexities, problems, and challenges that must be addressed by their generation.

My faith in God, humankind, and the future is unshakeable because I have met and supped with the peoples of the world. Everywhere there is a deep commitment to solving our mutual problems. I am convinced that together we can create a more peaceful, a more plentiful, and a more pleasing world.

Lloyd Lewan
Former Executive Dean, Semester at Sea
April 1985
Denver, Colorado

The History of Shipboard Education

Peace can never be kept by force,
it can only be achieved by understanding.
Albert Einstein

Voyages of discovery to distant lands and unknown peoples have captured the imagination of mankind from earliest time. Voyages heighten our awareness of both the diversity and the commonality of the human condition. Over and over again we learn that by sharing experiences with other cultures we discover ourselves. Voyages of learning and discovery continue today; and today, as throughout history, oceans provide the pathway. Since 1963 a special shipboard program has enriched the lives of thousands of young people by providing a globe-circling adventure in international education. First known as the University of the Seven Seas and then as World Campus Afloat, since 1977 this program has been called Semester at Sea.

Semester at Sea is far more than a travel adventure. It is a quest for knowledge about our world; it is a meaningful preparation for life; it is an eager investigation of universal ideas; and it is a close personal relationship built on international interests, between students and faculty. The program is based on the simple belief that the most effective way for students to develop into well-rounded individuals is through an organized educational experience that exposes them to the realities of our vast and varied world. It is precisely the kind of education about which Marshall McLuhan wrote,

> Someday all of us will spend our lives in our own school, the world. And education—in the sense of learning to love, to grow, to change—can become not woeful preparation for some job that makes us less than we could be, but the very essence, the joyful whole of existence itself.*

Travel can open eyes and minds; it can enhance respect for humankind and what we have created on this earth; it can change the way people view

each other and themselves. American astronauts, the ultimate travelers, reported experiences of an almost spiritual nature as they circled the earth. Frank Borman, one of these modern-day explorers, served as commander of Apollo 8, the first lunar mission. With this flight, man, for the first time ventured far enough into space to view the entire world. From lunar orbit Borman said, "There is a beautiful world out there." Back home, he was more specific.

> The view of the earth from the moon fascinated me—a small disk, 240,000 miles away. It was hard to think that little thing held so many frustrations. Raging nationalistic interests, famines, wars, pestilence don't show from that distance. . . . If some stranger came from another part of the heavens, he would certainly know instinctively . . . that the destinies of all who lived on it must inevitably be interwoven and joined. We are one hunk of ground, water, air, clouds, floating around in space. From out there it really is one world.**

Students who circumnavigate the globe during a Semester at Sea return with similar feelings. They learn that there is only one world, inhabited by one people. The problems that the world faces—no matter where they exist on the globe—are theirs to share, to understand, and to solve.

The men who laid the foundation of Semester at Sea would be very pleased with these results. These men were from different countries, different

*Quoted in Seymour Fersh, *Asia: Teaching About/Learning From* (New York, NY: Teachers College Press of Columbia University, 1978).

**Frank Borman, *A Science Fiction World—Awesome, Forlorn Beauty*, Life Magazine, January 17, 1969, p. 28.

cultures, and different generations, but they shared the same basic philosophy. They realized that it was not necessary for everyone to see things in the same way. What was important was that human beings understand how and why their differences exist. To these men, getting along together was a pure and simple matter of discovery and understanding. Education, they believed, should give students the means to discover and to understand. Ships that sailed the oceans of the world were the tools they used to implement this philosophy. The exceptional men who created shipboard education are linked by a series of fateful events and remarkable coincidences. To appreciate the Semester at Sea program of the 1980s, we must start with events that occurred many years earlier.

The first attempt to take a group of college students around the world by ship for the purpose of study and scientific investigation was made by an American, James O. Woodruff, Esq., of Indianapolis, Indiana. Woodruff, together with fellow promoter and former mayor of Indianapolis Daniel Macauley, hoped to turn a profit as well as break some new ground in American higher education. The voyage was scheduled to begin on October 1, 1877, from New York City; its purpose was "to study the arts, archaeology and present condition of better-known countries and the geology, geography, fauna and flora as well as the history and characters of the people, of those less-known." This ambitious undertaking had the approval of the federal government. The four year old steamship *Ontario* was secured for the planned two-year voyage. About four hundred students were to sail, together with a faculty who would be paid $5,000 each for their services. Despite elaborate planning, the voyage never took place. A lack of adequate student enrollment, and the death of Woodruff in 1879, led to the abandonment of what would have been the first voyage of a floating university.

Although a few attempts were made in the early 1900s to plan similar voyages, none ever came to pass. Most notable of these failed attempts was a voyage for boys, planned in 1901 by a young naval officer on the vessel *Young America*. The requirement of conforming to naval discipline was unpopular with the students, and resulted in the cancellation of the voyage. Another attempt at a world educational tour by ship was made by the American industrialist Asa Chandler shortly after World War I. Unfortunately, the navy transport he purchased from the government proved unsuitable, and this attempt was abandoned.

The end of World War I brought a surge of interest by Americans in the rest of the world. The many walls of provincialism were broken down on college campuses all over the country. Young soldiers and nurses returning from overseas discovered that their firsthand contact with the world had awakened their intellectual curiosity in a way classroom studies had never done. It was this climate that fostered the landmark event that occurred in the port of Yokohama, Japan in the early morning of November 5, 1926.

To the casual observer along the waterfront that cool autumn day, it was just another boatload of tourists coming to crowd the already busy streets of Yokohama. Nothing could have been further from the truth. To the 504 students on board the slowly moving steamship that had sailed from America a month before, and to the welcoming group of Japanese educational leaders who awaited them on the wharf, the event marked the inauguration of a brand new movement in liberal education, the floating university. The American students had arrived in Japan to begin their acquaintance with the peoples and civilizations of the Old World. Never before had the New World sent such a group of ambassadors. Representing the culture, traditions, and ideals of the West, these students made an impression upon the East that would have long-lasting effects. It was a memorable day, not only in the history of academic study, but also in the progress of international accord.

The triumph of November 5, 1926 belonged to one man. That date marked the culmination of years of hard work, belief in a cause, and innovative thought by James Edwin Lough of New York University. If anyone deserves to be called the Father of Shipboard Education, this is the man.

A portly, slightly balding man with a hearty laugh, James Lough was regarded with suspicion by his university colleagues. Some considered him a maverick, others "a visionary of rare degree." But all agreed that he was an innovator, and committed to making changes in American higher education. Lough was the product of a traditional education. He received a B.A. and an M.A. from Miami University in Ohio and a B.A., M.A., and Ph.D.

from Harvard. Lough began his teaching career at traditional schools like Radcliffe, Wellesley, and Harvard. Soon after joining the faculty of New York University as a professor of psychology in 1901, however, he came to believe that changes could and should be made in the traditional educational methods of American universities. He soon became a leader in a brand new movement in higher education, a movement to free students from the confines of textbooks, classrooms, and the lecture method. Travel and experience, he felt, should be added as useful and appropriate educational tools.

Lough put his philosophy to work. In 1908 he became dean of the Extramural Division of New York University, a division whose activities would extend beyond the walls of the campus. The new division first experimented with conducting courses in commerce and finance "on location" in the Wall Street district of New York, and art courses in the Metropolitan Museum of Art. In 1914 the division offered a summer course on European industrial education methods, sending a group of students across the Atlantic with one instructor. Dean Lough was pleased with the results of this popular course, which demonstrated that under proper guidance, travel experiences could be employed as laboratory material and that travel/study courses could be organized to conform to college standards and to confer college credits.

In the summer of 1920, Dean Lough led a group of students on a tour of Greece that followed the footsteps of Greece's ancient philosophers. During a visit to the University of Athens, he met a serious Greek student named Constantine Raises. Fluent in English, Raises became Lough's guide and interpreter that summer and on subsequent visits to Greece. Lough, standing an imposing six feet three, and Raises, barely five feet tall, were quite a contrast as they walked together among the ruins of Delphi and Olympia.

The friendship that developed between this prominent educator from the United States and the young Greek student would last a lifetime. It was a friendship based on mutual respect. Lough admired Raises' serious attitude, his sense of adventure, and the pure joy he found in learning. Raises marveled at Lough's knowledge of Greek history and at his ability to teach it. During the summers of 1920, 1921, and 1922, he watched Lough make that history come alive. He sensed the love Lough had for his students, and their deep affection for him. It was the first time this young university student had experienced formal education outside the classroom, but it would not be the last. This slightly built Greek would later play a giant's role in the

development of shipboard education in America.

In the 1920s, conditions in postwar Europe stabilized and the Extramural Division prospered. The division extended its operations to include travel/study tours in several European countries, as well as resident study courses based in France, Germany, Italy, and England. The tremendous positive student reaction to these European courses emboldened Dean Lough to begin thinking seriously about a more elaborate travel/study program. "Why just a summer program; why just Europe?", he thought. "Why not an entire academic year, and why not the world?"

Meanwhile, Constantine Raises had experienced some significant changes in his life. In 1922 he left the University of Athens and returned to his home town of Smyrna to join his father in the family import-export

James Edwin Lough, 1926   *Constantine Raises, 1930*

business. At that time the Greeks and the Turks were at war, and in September the Turkish army entered Smyrna. During the ensuing battle a fire broke out and this largely wooden city burned to the ground. Raises was among the 350,000 Greeks who were rescued by the Allies. Separated from his family and forced to live in a refugee camp, he became determined to emigrate to America. In November of 1922, he managed to set sail for the United States. Soon after arriving in New York he contacted his old friend Dean Lough, who helped him get settled and find a clerical job on the *New York World*. Although pleased to be employed, Raises found that his heart was not in journalism; he longed for a wider world. In 1924 he left his newspaper job and obtained a position as a purser on the *President Garfield*.

After a trip around-the-world, Raises found his life permanently changed. He became convinced of the mind-expanding value of travel to other lands, and committed himself to a career promoting the travel experience.

In May of 1924, not long after his second voyage on the *President Garfield*, Raises met Captain Felix Riesenberger, Commander of the New York Maritime Academy's schoolship, the *Newport*. Riesenberger was doing research for a book he was writing on the maritime history of the world. Raises was able to help him by translating a needed volume from Greek to English. Riesenberger was so impressed with the quality of Raises' work, and his obvious affection for ships and the sea, that he offered him a job as his personal aide on the next voyage of the *Newport*. Raises accepted, and overnight this twenty-four-year-old Greek was made an ensign in the New York Maritime Academy.

Raises made only one voyage—a brief trip to the Mediterranean—on the *Newport*, but for him it was an important journey. He saw the impact the voyage had on the young cadets as they met the peoples of the Mediterranean. He saw the cadets come to realize that there were really two worlds—one they could measure with their sextants and rules, and one they could feel with their hearts and minds. It was during this voyage that he asked himself, "If Maritime cadets can have a schoolship, why can't 'regular' students have a similar ship?"

On his return to New York, Raises contacted Dean Lough to discuss the subject. In the first of a number of astonishing coincidences that have marked the development of shipboard education, Lough told Raises that he was already planning an around-the-world voyage for college students. What he needed was someone to help finance the world's first floating university. Raises knew immediately that he wanted to help plan the voyage, and to sail on it as well. He also knew someone with money enough to back it—Andrew J. McIntosh, a trustee of the New York Maritime Academy. A wealthy Quaker and retired shipping broker, McIntosh had a sincere desire to do something that would advance the cause of world peace. Raises was certain that McIntosh would love the idea of a floating university. He was right.

Raises discussed the concept of a floating university with Captain Riesenberger. The Captain was genuinely enthusiastic about the idea and offered to help. In early 1925 he gave a dinner party on board the *Newport* to generate interest in a floating university for college students. Among the guests he invited were James Lough, Andrew McIntosh, Constantine Raises, Herbert Swope (managing editor of the *New York World*), and representatives of the Holland America Line. It was unanimous among those in the Captain's dining quarters that the idea had merit and should be pursued. To the utter amazement of Dean Lough, McIntosh handed him a check for $25,000, made out to the still nonexistent "Floating University." Raises and Lough were jubilant. They left the *Newport* that evening feeling secure that the first American floating university had been launched.

An organization called the University Travel Association, Inc. (UTA) was soon formed to plan the voyage. With McIntosh serving as president, Lough as director of educational affairs, and Raises in charge of the around-the-world itinerary, it was UTA's goal to begin the voyage in September of 1925. The planning went well. A charter was received from the New York Department of Education to operate a university on board a ship. Dean Lough persuaded New York University to give its full support to the project. A faculty and staff of sixty agreed to sail without pay. Herbert Swope wrote a glowing article in the *World*, giving the project much-needed publicity. Most important, the Holland America Line offered, for the token fee of one dollar, the use of a ship that was sitting idle in Rotterdam. Preparations began immediately to make the SS *Ryndam*, a 13,000 ton, coal-burning steamship that had survived a German mine in the North Atlantic, ready for the historic journey. All the planning went for naught. Too few students registered for the voyage, forcing Dean Lough to announce a one-year postponement.

New York University was embarrassed by the delay of the voyage. Further, many of the university's faculty did not support Dean Lough's unconventional methods. As a consequence, in March of 1926, New York University withdrew its support for the voyage. This was a major blow to Lough, who resigned as dean of the Extramural Division and took a one-year leave of absence. NYU's withdrawal from the project turned out to be a blessing in disguise. Now that UTA was independent and no longer affiliated with any one college, other schools more freely provided their cooperation and support. Applications began pouring in from all across the country. Able to work full-time on the voyage, Lough redoubled his efforts to make his dream of a floating university come true. His work brought rewards; student berths were soon filled, and more than 200 applicants were turned away.

The *Ryndam* set sail from a Hoboken, New Jersey pier on September

18, 1926 with a full quota of 504 students and a faculty and administrative staff of 63. It was an exciting sailing; the *Ryndam* was decorated with flags from stem to stern. Many of the thousands who lined the Fifth Street pier seeing their loved ones off got caught up in the spirit of the moment and tried to book passage themselves. Tears were abundant as the harbor tugs nudged the *Ryndam* out to sea and on its way to Yokohama via the Panama Canal. The students, representing 143 colleges, came from forty states as well as Canada, Cuba, and Hawaii. Among the faculty was Henry J. Allen, a former Governor of Kansas, who edited the ship's newspaper, *The Binnacle*. The crew of 256 was mostly Dutch. In what must have been his proudest moment, James Lough sailed as dean of the voyage. The position of cruise director was filled by Constantine Raises.

The story of the seven and a half month odyssey of the SS *Ryndam* would fill volumes. The ship covered forty-one thousand miles and visited thirty-five countries and more than ninety cities, including Shanghai, Hong Kong, Manila, Bangkok, Columbo, Bombay, Haifa, Venice, Gibraltar, Lisbon, and Oslo. Students selected from the ninety-five courses offered. Mere statistics, however, do not do justice to the true significance of this pioneering voyage. For the first time in American higher education, an entire college had become mobile. On September 18, 1926 a complete campus—including faculty, students, gymnasium, classrooms, dormitories, cafeteria, library, and laboratories, all housed on the decks of the *Ryndam*—set itself in motion around the world for the sole purpose of world education. The voyage was considered an academic success. As faculty member Dr. Douglas Ridgley put it, "The trip provided exceptional educational returns for the students." The vast majority of the students agreed, calling the voyage "the greatest educational experience of our lives."

Many of the students from that first experimental voyage gathered on September 18, 1976 on the *Queen Mary* Hotel in Long Beach, California to celebrate the golden anniversary of their original sailing. Even fifty years later they still spoke in glowing terms of their experience and how it influenced them to think in terms of "living in the world, not just America," and of how it changed their lives. The celebrants reminisced well into the night, speaking of events that had taken place half a century earlier as though they had occurred that very day.

They remembered how Jack Morgan had spent his pocket money for the entire voyage in Japan; and they recalled that his cable home was a marvel of succinctness: "SEND JACK CASH."

They remembered a man named Benito Mussolini and the reception he had given them in Rome.

They remembered Professor Raber and the geology expedition he led to the top of Mt. Fuji in the dead of winter.

They remembered the consternation and the horror of the first glimpse of their "cabins"—6′ by 6′ by 6′ partitioned cubicles in the hold of the ship; they remembered that two people shared each cubicle, and that "tall fellows had to sleep with bent knees."

They remembered the smell peculiar to those cubicles—a unique mixture of spices and sea, tar, dirt, and rusty iron.

They remembered the two swimming pools, homemade wooden structures 15′ by 25′ lined with canvas, which sat on top of the deck.

They remembered that the men outnumbered the women by four to one.

They remembered their sincere concern for the crew, who had to endure the intense heat of the engine room; and they remembered the many nights they volunteered to help shovel coal into the boilers.

The SS Ryndam in Venice, Italy—February 1927

And they remembered Dean Lough's characterization of the voyage and the goals he set on the first day at sea: "This shall not be a mere sightseeing tour, but a college year of educational travel and systematic study: to develop an interest in foreign affairs, to train students to think in world terms, and to strengthen international understanding and good will."

And they all agreed that Dean Lough's goals had been met.

Conflict and strife among the advocates of shipboard education clouded the years following the *Ryndam's* triumphant return to Hoboken in May of 1927. Dean Lough's liberal approach to education and his involvement with privately financed student tours had been a source of continuous irritation to NYU. Instead of receiving acclaim from his university when he returned from the *Ryndam* voyage, Lough found that he had been permanently discharged. After twenty-seven years of service to NYU, this was a severe personal disappointment. And that was not the only bad news awaiting Lough.

Andrew McIntosh, the principal financial backer of the *Ryndam* program, had developed his own idea of how the floating university should function. It differed so significantly from Lough's that McIntosh left UTA and set up his own organization, called International University Cruise, Inc. (IUC). McIntosh persuaded Raises to join him in the new venture. Lough did not view Raises' association with McIntosh as a violation of their friendship; the two continued to share information about the different approaches to international education, and later worked together on other voyages.

McIntosh's organization, influenced by his own Quaker background, arranged stays of two to four weeks in selected ports, allowing students to actually live among the people of differing cultures. In spite of disrupting the formal shipboard classroom work, McIntosh believed this was the only way that true cross-cultural understanding could be achieved. So it was that in the summer of 1927 there were two organizations based in New York City set up to operate floating universities. The rivalry between UTA and IUC resulted in neither organization attracting enough students to send out a voyage in the

fall of 1927, but it wasn't for lack of trying. Both organizations had faculties in place, itineraries planned, advertising campaigns implemented, and ships secured. However, fewer than 300 students between the two organizations enrolled, and both plans were scrapped. Later that year McIntosh became ill and resigned the presidency of IUC. He was succeeded by the noted historian, author, and lecturer Sydney Greenbie. Both Greenbie and Lough were determined to launch a floating university voyage that would start with the fall semester of 1928, and both succeeded. Not one but two ships sailed out of New York harbor that fall dedicated to university-level education.

Of the two voyages, the one made by Greenbie received more publicity in the world press. This was in large measure due to the enthusiasm of the cruise director, who was continually granting interviews in port. This man was making his fourth trip around the world since 1924—Constantine Raises. Raises, and Greenbie too, made certain the press found out about the audience George Bernard Shaw had given members of the student body while in London. They also made sure the press learned of an incident that occurred in a New Delhi train station, an incident that remains one of the most dramatic in the history of shipboard education.

From an uncomfortable, third-class day coach, a man emerged from among the peasants squatting with their bundles, babies, and food to greet the students of the floating university. The students recognized him immediately as one of the famous men of their time, Mohandas K. Gandhi. They talked to him and shook his hand. His words were few and conventional. He told them to read *Mother India* and then to use their own eyes as they traveled in his country. He answered the questions of some about the symbolic burning of foreign cloth in the Indian independence movement. He spoke to others sympathetically of their student interests and their desire to see the world firsthand. But it was his magnetic personality and presence, more than his words, that left a lasting impression. They could sense how this simple little man was able to have such supreme influence among his people.

Gandhi waved a kindly goodbye as his train pulled out for Calcutta. A few minutes later the students boarded a train headed in the opposite direction for Bombay. When they arrived in Bombay they read in the newspapers of Gandhi's arrest in Calcutta because his followers had burned foreign cloth in a public square. The whole experience, brief and casual as it was, had given these young Americans a feeling that they had been very near to one of the most dramatic political and social movements of their time.*

The Gandhi experience and the voyage as a whole made a lasting impression on Greenbie. Like McIntosh before him, he had his own ideas on the concept of travel for education, and wanted to strike out on his own. In the spring of 1929 he left IUC and founded another student travel/study program he dubbed "Traversity." He made it clear that his Traversity was not a "Sea-versity." Students would go around the world, but the cost of maintaining an exclusive ship was eliminated. Instead, the new plan used trains and regular passenger ships.

With Greenbie now working on a new theme, Lough merged IUC and UTA into one organization, applying the name University Travel Association, Inc. to both. In September of 1929 the reorganized UTA headed by Lough, began a series of floating university voyages that was to last seven years. When the SS *Hirondelle* sailed back to New York on June 26, 1936, the faculty and students were still exhausted from final exams. They did not know that their voyage, which had taken them to thirty-one ports around the world, marked the end of an era. Not even Constantine Raises, who was the *Hirondelle's* cruise director, had any way of knowing that this would be his last voyage on a floating university. War clouds that loomed over Europe were about to bring an end to Lough's work, taking young college students on long ocean voyages around the world would no longer be safe. For the next twenty-two years of economic instability and hot and cold war, floating universities did not sail.

In 1958 a Whittier, California dentist, Dr. Gerald S. Black, had just been elected president of his local Rotary Club. A deeply religious man, he asked his pastor to pray with him so that he might gain enlightenment toward the creation of a more peaceful world. More than anything else, Black wanted his Rotary Club to take some direct, meaningful action that would contribute to

*"The Ghandi Incident" was paraphrased from *Marco Polo* Gazette, Vol. 1, No. 1, April 1929, page 2. Published in Cairo, Egypt by the Floating University.

world peace during his term as president. Soon after his "prayer for peace," Dr. Black established a special Rotary Club committee on world problems and solutions. To head this committee he selected William T. Hughes, a local Whittier businessman. Hughes would later joke, "I don't know who made the mistake, Dr. Black or God, but I got the job." As things turned out, no mistake had been made—Black could not have chosen a better man.

Born in northern California in 1895, Bill Hughes had one year of college education. It was his drive, optimistic outlook on life, and common sense that made him successful and prosperous. During the course of his career he had been a restaurant owner, land developer, tile manufacturer, real estate broker, and in 1958 was the owner of a plumbing supply business in Whittier.

Hughes took his new appointment seriously. He wanted to develop a realistic proposal that would allow his Rotary Club to make a contribution toward strengthening good will among nations. Actually, Bill Hughes had been working in Rotary along these lines for some time. Since 1953 he had been director of his club's Visiting International Student Activities (VISA) program. His work with young people from many backgrounds and cultures had made him aware of the importance of exchanging ideas among the people of the world through person-to-person contact. While on a business trip to Washington, D.C. in 1959, Hughes met with his congressman, Representative George Kasem. They discussed the VISA program and shared their mutual interest in people-to-people programs. They also shared their enthusiasm for an idea that might be the ultimate in such programs—an international university, perhaps even one established on a ship that could sail from country to country. Such a university would allow students to study world problems by direct observation. The more Bill Hughes thought about it, the more he liked the idea. When he returned to Whittier, Hughes decided to propose the idea of a floating university to his Rotary Club. Bill Hughes had never heard of James E. Lough, the SS *Ryndam*, or anything else about the shipboard education movement that had begun in 1925. But that would soon change.

The Whittier Rotary Club split on Hughes' idea. Many members supported the idea immediately, while others felt it would be too big a project for their small club to undertake. Rotary attorneys believed that the possible liabilities associated with an ocean-going campus would be prohibitive. Hughes was advised that if he wanted to pursue the idea, he would have to do so outside the formal Rotary International structure. The club could endorse and support the idea, but could not formally sponsor it.

Hughes had a difficult decision to make. Should he proceed on his own with what he felt in his heart was a good idea? He received some unexpected help in making his decision. As he was reading the newspaper one evening, a story about the life of a San Francisco travel agent caught his eye. The story told about the adventures of a man who had visited more than 190 countries and had, in the 1920s, played an important role in the development of international education through the use of ships. Bill Hughes wasted no time in getting to San Francisco and meeting with Constantine Raises.

Over lunch at the Mark Hopkins Hotel, Hughes heard the story of the *Ryndam's* voyage and of the shipboard education programs that had taken place before World War II. Raises spoke so enthusiastically about the voyages, and about the quality of learning that had taken place, that Bill Hughes knew he must proceed. Hughes asked Constantine to suggest a name for this new venture—something fresh, something inspiring. Constantine thought for a moment and then said, "Why don't you call it the 'University of the Seven Seas'?" Hughes could not convince Raises to move to Los Angeles and join him in developing this program, but Raises did accept an appointment as special advisor to the University of the Seven Seas, and agreed to act as its spokesman in northern California.

Hughes formed a committee of educators and other prominent citizens to begin the monumental task of organizing and building a university. The committee persuaded Representative Kasem to introduce a resolution in the U.S. House of Representatives endorsing the idea of a floating university. By April of 1960, articles of incorporation had been filed with the State of California for the "University of the Seven Seas." In March of 1961, the university became an independent legal entity authorized under California law to conduct a program of higher education. Dr. Ray Nichols, a speech professor at Whittier College, was elected president of the university, and Bill Hughes was elected president of the board of trustees. Serving on the board was Dr. James Price, former chancellor of the University of Denver and student body president on the 1926 *Ryndam* voyage. Other members included Olympic gold medalist Rafer Johnson; the president of Chi Hai University of Hong Kong, Lan Shu Wong; and the owners of the food processing firm Laura Scudder's, Inc., Jack and Valarie Scudder. But America's

newest university had a long way to go. It still had no faculty, no campus, and no students.

Finding good people to work and to support the university proved to be much easier than finding a suitable ship. Hughes hoped that one might be obtained at little or no cost from the mothball fleet of the U.S. Maritime Administration. He soon learned that even if he received such a ship as a gift, the cost of making it ready for service as a university would be prohibitive. The idea of purchasing a ship was replaced by the financially more realistic proposal of chartering a ship from a commercial shipping line. It took about three years of searching and negotiating with various shipping companies before a ship was actually chartered. The company that finally provided the new floating campus turned out to be the same one that had supplied the very first floating university nearly forty years earlier.

The Holland America Line had never completely forgotten its educational experiment with Dean Lough in 1926. Line executives felt that with Europe's recovery from the war complete, and with the easing of cold war tensions, it was time for another try at a floating university. By a remarkable coincidence, when Hughes first contacted them, the Holland America Line had available through a subsidiary company a 12,574-ton passenger ship named the MS *Seven Seas*.

This ship, built in Chester, Pennsylvania in 1940 as a dry goods and livestock vessel, had a colorful past. When World War II broke out and the Navy could not wait to build aircraft carriers from the keel up, she was purchased by the U.S. government and converted into an escort aircraft carrier—the first of her kind. Christened the USS *Long Island*, she was given a flight deck and antiaircraft guns. This "baby flat top," with her small convoy of thirty planes, served as the backstop for the main American forces during the battle of Midway Island. Her catapulted aircraft flew cover for a force of surface warships during this historic battle in June of 1942. Following her decommissioning in 1946, she was converted to a passenger liner and served as an immigrant ship, sailing between Italy and Australia. In 1953 she was rebuilt, renamed the MS *Seven Seas*, and bought by a Holland America Line subsidiary. When Hughes found her, she was a transatlantic passenger liner, registered in Bremen and staffed by a West German crew.

In February of 1963 a charter contract was signed and preparations begun to create a university on board the *Seven Seas*. It was very pleasing for

Bill Hughes to realize that the hanger deck of this one-time carrier, once teeming with the instruments of war, would now be inhabited by students. It was a happy paradox for all connected with this new university that this ship that had fought in a war caused by lack of understanding among people would now contribute to the growth of understanding.

In contrast to the original *Ryndam's* seven and a half month voyage, which encompassed an entire academic year, the University of the Seven Seas planned journeys to last no longer than a single semester, about three and a half months. Hughes was hopeful that the *Seven Seas* would sail every semester on a different around-the-world itinerary. The university also planned to build a land campus near San Diego, in the city of Ramona. San Diego was to become the home port for the *Seven Seas*. The campus would serve as a world resource and liberal arts center where students would prepare in teams for their voyage around the world. A regular four-year degree program was envisioned, with all students required to make at least one voyage. These were ambitious plans for a new and unique university with limited finances. Because there were no endowments and no alumni, its existence depended on the number of students and benefactors it could attract.

With Dr. Woodrow Whitten of California Western University as dean of the ship, the *Seven Seas* sailed from New York on October 22, 1963. This first voyage of the *Seven Seas* marked the reawakening of a movement that had come to a halt in 1936. Although only 275 students sailed, it was a 110-day voyage that none would forget. Like their predecessors on the *Ryndam* thirty-seven years before, the students were received by their foreign hosts with great ceremony, and acclaimed pioneers of a new era of international education and friendship. Of the many places they visited, none would forget Monte Carlo and the address given them by Jacques Cousteau on the importance of preserving the oceans; the Red Sea, where the *Seven Seas* dropped anchor over the continental shelf so that the oceanography class could scuba dive and collect samples; or Viet Nam and the U.S. Army helicopter escorts that kept an eye out for snipers as they sailed up the Saigon River. And none would ever forget Saigon itself, where they saw young men preparing for war.

Bill Hughes, who was able to sail on the inaugural voyage, would not forget it either. Wherever he went, he was hailed as an educational pioneer. In Hong Kong he attended a reception given for him by leading Chinese

businessmen. Hughes recalled later that one of the men he met seemed to have more than just a passing interest in the floating university idea. The man spoke enthusiastically about the educational merits of the University of the Seven Seas, and offered his help should it ever be needed. The man's name was C. Y. Tung, and he would soon play a pivotal role in advancing the cause of shipboard education.

The University of the Seven Seas did not survive. Its second, and last, around-the-world journey took place as the fall semester of 1964–65. Although the university was authorized by the state of California to issue transcripts and award diplomas, it was never fully accredited by the Western Association of Schools and Colleges. This prevented the university from assuring students that their credits would be transferable to, or even recognized by, any other school. The problems of accreditation and low student enrollment were the primary causes of the demise of the university. Plans for the spring 1965 around-the-world voyage were abandoned. The few students who had already enrolled were provided with the less costly alternative of an in-depth semester in Europe. The students who chose this alternative sailed on the *Seven Seas* from San Diego to Southampton, in March of 1965.

As the *Seven Seas* sailed toward Southampton, the fate of the university was under serious review. Hughes agreed with his colleagues that the floating university could survive only if it were to become part of an already accredited, land-based college, a notion that Dean Lough had discarded some thirty years earlier. Thus Hughes, with the full support of the Holland America Line, began his search for a permanent home base and academic sponsor.

At the urging of Seven Seas' Trustees Jack and Valerie Scudder, Hughes contacted Chapman College in Orange, California. The Scudders had sailed on the first voyage of the *Seven Seas* and had become enthusiastic supporters of the program. Valerie Scudder was a graduate of Chapman College and knew President John L. Davis well. She was convinced that Chapman College would profit from associating with the Seven Seas program. Fortunately, Davis agreed with her. An imaginative and progressive leader, Davis believed that taking on the Seven Seas program would expand Chapman's vision and give it a dimension unique among American colleges and universities.

In March of 1965 the faculty of this small, private, liberal arts institution approved the idea, and in May the Chapman trusteees gave it their endorsement. The college became fully responsible for all aspects of the academic program aboard the *Seven Seas*. The organization known as the University of the Seven Seas ceased to function as an educational institution, but remained in existence as a foundation, still headed by Bill Hughes. The Seven Seas Division of Chapman College was established. Dr. Netter Worthington, an art professor at Chapman, was selected to head this new division and to serve as dean of the ship on the first Chapman voyage.

On October 20, 1965 the *Seven Seas* sailed from New York on a 108-day semester that included visits to sixteen ports in Europe, the Middle East, India, and Asia. This voyage marked the beginning of a period of shipboard education by Chapman College that was to last ten years. It proved to be a crucial period. Under Chapman's direction, shipboard education was solidified in America as a well-developed, viable option for college students interested in international education. Twenty-one consecutive semester voyages were made. Well over nine thousand students participated in what Chapman boasted was a "direct opportunity to observe the contemporary world scene, to come to a firsthand knowledge of nations, and to enter appreciatively into the cultural heritage of other people."

Of the twenty-one voyages, only the first two were made by the *Seven Seas*. In 1966 the Holland America Line made a newer and larger ship available to Chapman. By one more happy coincidence, it bore the same name as the first floating university, the SS *Ryndam*. With the acquisition of this new ship, Chapman renamed the program World Campus Afloat (WCA) and placed it organizationally in the Chapman College Division of International Studies. Dr. M. A. Griffiths, a Chapman graduate, was later appointed by President Davis to administer the program. A history professor

William T. Hughes, 1964

C. Y. Tung, 1934

and academic dean of the college, Dr. Griffith's selection as vice president for international studies began an association with shipboard education that would last well beyond the life of World Campus Afloat.

The new *Ryndam*, originally named the *Dinteldyk*, had been built in 1950. She started her sailing life as an immigrant ship bringing people from all parts of Europe to New York and Canada. It was not uncommon for this 15,000 ton, eight-decked liner to carry over 800 immigrants on her transatlantic runs. Later she would carry regular passengers as a moderately priced cruise ship. Never more than 600 students sailed on any one voyage on the *Ryndam* during her years as Chapman's floating campus. Life on board the *Ryndam* for these students was much different than for the ship's earlier passengers. Males and females were housed on different decks. Only on weekends could men and women visit each other's cabins. A strict behavior code was observed in port as well. Students could stay off the ship overnight only if written permission was obtained from the dean.

Each semester a curriculum of about a hundred courses was offered. The courses were designed for undergraduate students, with emphasis on the humanities and social studies. A few adaptable courses such as marine

Above: The SS Ryndam, 1968. Right: The RMS Queen Elizabeth

biology and oceanography were included. All were developed to assure full credit transfer to the students' home universities. Professors were selected not only from the Chapman faculty, but from colleges and universities throughout the United States and the world as well. Deans for the voyages were generally selected from the faculty of Chapman's Division of Inter-

national Studies. Drs. Ed Alderson and Lloyd Lewan became the two most prominent deans for a decade. Academically, World Campus Afloat slowly began to gain respectability; but financially it was never on an even keel.

From its inception, the costs of operating WCA far outstripped its revenues. Most of the deficits were assumed by the Holland America Line. John Dutilh, the Line's managing director, felt strongly about the value of the program in international terms. At his direction, the Line established a scholarship program that provided financial assistance for up to twenty-five students each semester. However, by 1970 it became apparent that the *Ryndam* needed major renovations to keep it operating. Costs for the work were estimated at between two and four million dollars. Because of the large amount of money involved, the Holland America Line could not agree to finance the needed work; Chapman College could not afford the expense. The college, determined to keep WCA alive, set out to find a new ship. There were many at Chapman who felt the end of World Campus Afloat was near. It was at this point that a quiet and extraordinary man stepped forward to offer a solution. He was C. Y. Tung of Hong Kong.

Born in Shanghai in 1912, his given name, Chao-Yung, meant "heralding fame and prosperity." No name could have been more prophetic. "C. Y.," as he came to be known, did not have a career in the normal sense of the word. His life was instead a series of risks, commitments, adventures, and successes. In 1930, the teenaged C. Y. Tung worked as a shipping clerk for the Tientsin Navigation Company. By 1970, he had risen to become one of the world's leading independent shipowners. His vast fleet included more than 150 ships, totaling more than eleven million tons. It was the world's most diversified fleet, including oil tankers, oil product carriers, container ships, and passenger liners. Under the trade name Orient Overseas Line, his freight and passenger liners called regularly in every major world port. Tung became regarded as a shipowner's shipowner. He had strong personal feelings about his ships, and made it a habit to visit them as often as possible. A man with a formidable memory, Tung could greet most of his hundreds of officers by name. He was often reluctant to sell elderly ships because he considered them old friends.

C. Y. Tung's adventures were not confined to the sea. He became an international banker, a major computer distributor in the Far East, an award-winning film maker, and a world-renowned patron of the arts. Despite his vast wealth, he lived a modest life. He neither smoked nor drank, and rose early each morning to spend an hour meditating before his breakfast of hot water with lemon. With friends from all walks of life, C. Y. lived his famous motto, "The greatest ship is friendship." He was also a firm believer in the value of education. In 1969, when Secretary General U Thant called on the United Nations to create an international university, C. Y. was among the first to support the concept. It was this man for all seasons who, on learning of Chapman's need for a new ship, came to the rescue.

On August 30, 1970 Tung met with representatives of World Campus Afloat, including Drs. Lewan and Alderson, to discuss the needs and objectives of their program. At that meeting, Mr. Tung expressed his hope that someday a truly international university could be created on board a ship, where students of different races, lifestyles, and cultures could live, study, and relax together. Tung hoped that his support for World Campus Afloat would provide the strength for such a university. Within weeks of this meeting, Mr. Tung established and funded the Seawise Foundation, Ltd., a nonprofit corporation. The purpose of this organization was to purchase a ship and immediately convert it to a floating university for the use of World

Campus Afloat. Within days, one of Tung's representatives called Chapman to announce, "We have a ship for you." And what a ship it was! Tung's Seawise Foundation had purchased the largest passenger ship ever built, RMS *Queen Elizabeth I.*

Launched in September of 1938, the *Queen Elizabeth* was the pride of the British Maritime fleet. During World War II, she transported nearly a million Allied troops to and from battle zones, sometimes carrying an entire division of fifteen thousand men at one time. Hitler offered the Iron Cross and $200,000 to the U-boat commander who could sink her. After the war she was refitted by the Cunard Line for passenger service, and for twenty years made weekly transatlantic crossings between Southampton and New York. By the end of the 1960s rapidly increasing operational costs and decreasing passenger counts forced the Cunard Line to retire her. She was purchased in 1968 by a group of Philadelphia businessmen and taken to Port Everglades, Florida to become a tourist attraction. This venture ended in bankruptcy. When the Seawise Foundation bought her for $3.2 million in September of 1970, this historic liner was languishing in the Florida sun.

C. Y. Tung planned a future for the *Queen Elizabeth* that would be worthy of her proud past. Tung renamed her the SS *Seawise University*, and together with Chapman College made elaborate plans for her as a replacement for the *Ryndam*. Tung directed that the old *Queen Elizabeth* be taken to Hong Kong for complete refurbishing. Fate dictated that this would be her last voyage. Thirty years of hard service and three and a half million miles, followed by years of neglect, had wreaked havoc on her boilers. In February of 1971, as she began her voyage to Hong Kong, one of her six boilers went out even before the harbor pilot was off the ship. Two days later, some twenty miles off Haiti, other boilers of the once mighty *Queen Elizabeth* blew. She lay adrift for forty-eight hours. A pair of tug boats managed to get the liner to Aruba, where Chinese technicians and spare parts were flown in from Hong Kong. Five months later the SS *Seawise University* limped into Hong Kong harbor, and a complete refitting of the ship began.

By the end of 1971, and well behind schedule, six million dollars had been spent on making the old *Queen Eliabeth* suitable for use as a floating university. Final hull repairs were to be done in dry dock in Japan. By early January of 1972 the SS *Seawise University* was ready to sail to Japan. With no stewards yet on board, a local catering firm was hired to provide a cocktail party for dockworkers and their families. On January 9 a fire broke out in the galley and spread unchecked throughout the ship. Two hundred workers and three hundred guests were evacuated and the SS *Seawise University* burned like a torch through the night. Firemen used fire engines mounted on ferry boats, as well as fireboats, in an effort to save the vessel. Their efforts were in vain. On the morning of January 10 all that remained of the SS *Seawise University* was a gutted, smoldering hulk. C. Y. Tung's plans to refit one of the greatest ships ever built into an international floating university were destroyed forever. Despite this tragedy, his commitment to international education and to shipboard education remained strong.

The SS Seawise University burning in Hong Kong Harbor, 1972

Because of the delays in refitting the *Queen Elizabeth*, in 1971 Tung had also purchased the liner *Atlantic* from the American Export Line and made it available to Chapman as an interim campus. He renamed the ship the SS *Universe Campus*. When he found her, she had been laid up in a Baltimore shipyard since 1968. The effort to bring this ship, inactive for four years, up to safety and operational standards in the few short months before the scheduled fall 1971 sailing was a great feat of Chinese know-how, team work, and dedication. Its name shortened to the SS *Universe*, this ship became home to thousands of college students in the 1970s and 1980s.

It was one more coincidence that this ship had been built by the same company that built the MS *Seven Seas*, the Sun Shipbuilding Company of Chester, Pennsylvania. Launched as the cargo ship *Badger Mariner* in 1953, she was later refitted as a passenger liner and renamed the *Atlantic*. The

furthest thing from a luxury liner, she had a wonderfully informal way about her. Perhaps more than any other ship used as a floating campus in the past, the SS *Universe* was loved by the students and faculty who roamed her decks. She became known affectionately as the "Great White Mother." Had it not been for the sudden demise of the *Queen Elizabeth*, this ship would never have played such an important part in the lives of so many students.

The SS *Universe* played an important part in the life of C. Y. Tung as well. Of all the ships in his huge fleet, this thirty-year-old, 18,000 ton, converted cargo ship was the one he came to love the most. He visited the ship often. It was not uncommon for him to drop in on students in Jakarta or Caracas or Manila or elsewhere along the itinerary of a voyage. He enjoyed talking to students and they to him. The students told him of the quality of their on-board classes and the excitement of meeting people around the world. His belief in shipboard education was reinforced; he recognized that his SS *Universe* was truly a special ship—a ship with a mission unlike any other sailing the oceans of the world. The SS *Universe*, supported by C. Y. Tung and the Seawise Foundation, ushered shipboard education into the decade of the Eighties. But it wasn't smooth sailing all the way. Unforeseen events and rough seas lay ahead that would test not only the SS *Universe* but also the very viability of shipboard education.

The fall 1975 sailing was the ninth consecutive global voyage for Chapman College. For all on board it proved to be one of the most difficult. The death of a popular Chinese crew member in a freak engine room accident created an atmosphere of melancholy throughout the ship. This air of despondency was compounded half way through the voyage. As the *Universe* steamed toward Beirut, news from California reached the ship that this was the last World Campus Afloat voyage. Chapman College, it was rumored, was going to drop the program. The economic recession of the mid-seventies caused Chapman's enrollments to drop severely. By the fall of 1975, the college was reordering its financial priorities and making substantial cuts in its operation. Chapman's financial and personnel resources were no longer able to provide an adequate base for World Campus Afloat. The decision was made to terminate the program.

As the *Universe* made her way toward Florida in December of 1975, all on board felt that they were witnessing the end of a special period of American higher education. No one really expected the ship to sail again as a floating university. The activity on board was keyed to dismantling this once-proud division of the Chapman campus. Students and faculty helped pack library books, academic records, laboratory equipment, and other Chapman property for shipment back to California. The faculty on board were united in their support of World Campus Afloat. Faculty member John Holloway, a lawyer affiliated with the University of Colorado in Boulder, made a personal commitment to keep shipboard education viable.

Two men at Chapman College also felt a strong commitment to the unique value of shipboard education. They knew of no other educational program demonstrating that the destinies of all who live on this planet are inextricably interwoven. They had seen hundreds of students come off the *Ryndam* and the *Universe* having learned that world problems are not someone else's, but their own. Firmly dedicated to the goals of shipboard education, Dr. M. A. Griffiths and a young WCA administrator, Dr. John Tymitz, decided to find a way to keep the *Universe* sailing as a floating university. Early in 1976, Griffiths and Tymitz, with the encouragement and financial backing of C. Y. Tung, set up a nonprofit educational corporation called the Institute for Shipboard Education. Having discovered the phrase "semester at sea" in descriptive literature about World Campus Afloat, they decided to call the program of study aboard the SS *Universe* "Semester at Sea." Tung, Tymitz, and Griffiths had a ship and a new name for their program, but no academic sponsor.

Upon his return to the University of Colorado campus, John Holloway began campaigning for the *Universe* program among influential faculty members. With strong support from the faculty and administration, Chancellor Russell Nelson made the decision to give his university's academic certification to the new Semester at Sea program. In the spring of 1976, academic affiliation was formalized between the Institute for Shipboard Education and the University of Colorado at Boulder. Under the agreement, the Institute retained financial and administrative responsibility for the program. The University of Colorado had the responsibility to establish the curriculum, approve the faculty, grant academic credit, and issue transcripts for all participants. In addition, the University would place an academic dean on each voyage.

Meanwhile, Mr. Tung had appointed Dr. Griffiths to serve as the first executive director of the Institute for Shipboard Education. It was Griffiths'

job to get the program up and running again. Chapman's termination of World Campus Afloat had received wide publicity throughout the country. Students needed to know that shipboard education, now accredited by the University of Colorado, was continuing on board the SS *Universe*. Griffiths launched a nationwide publicity and student recruiting campaign. And, in a key decision, he hired former WCA Dean Lloyd Lewan to join the Institute as its director of academic affairs on the Boulder campus. It was Griffiths, Tymitz, and Lewan who, in addition to alternating as deans on the early Semester at Sea voyages, formed the nucleus of the Institute. These three men gave shipboard education the stability it needed to grow and prosper.

M. A. Griffiths   *Lloyd S. Lewan*   *John P. Tymitz*

It had been a year and a half since the *Universe* had sailed, but now, in the spring of 1977, she was ready again. With 438 students on board and Deans Morris Massey of the University of Colorado and John Tymitz of the Institute for Shipboard Education in charge, a new era was ushered in as the *Universe* sailed from Los Angeles on the very first Semester at Sea voyage.

The Semester at Sea program enjoyed tremendous popularity on the Boulder campus. It was not uncommon for the University to have over a hundred of its own students on board the *Universe* on any given voyage. But the academic marriage between the Institute and the University did not last. With the end of the fall 1980 voyage, Colorado's sponsorship of the program came to a close. A dispute over who should have dominant control of the program could not be resolved to the satisfaction of both parties. As a result, the fall 1980 voyage of the SS *Universe* marked the last in a series of seven around-the-world voyages under the academic aegis of the University of Colorado. The two institutions parted company amicably, and the three-year-old Semester at Sea program was once again without an academic sponsor.

Due to the diligent efforts of Drs. Griffiths and Lewan, Semester at Sea was not orphaned for long. Its academic reputation and popularity with students made it an attractive option for a number of American colleges and universities. After evaluating several applicants, the Institute's board of trustees accepted the proposal of the University of Pittsburgh to contract as the academic sponsor. Pittsburgh could provide the program with stronger international support by establishing it within their widely respected Center for International Studies. It also provided the opportunity for the program to broaden its student population from eastern colleges and universities. Led by its president, Dr. Wesley Posvar, the University committed itself to establishing an academic program of the highest caliber onboard the *Universe*. In 1981 a formal agreement was signed; the Semester at Sea Program had an academic home once again.

The University of Pittsburgh made good on its commitment. President Posvar appointed Dr. Keith McDuffie to act as liaison between the University and Semester at Sea. In the spring of 1981 Dr. McDuffie and Dr. Griffiths began a series of globe-circling voyages on the *Universe* that were unparalleled in academic excellence. Everyone connected with the Institute felt secure that the program had finally found a permanent base. With close to two thousand students having sailed on the first four Pittsburgh voyages, the future looked bright for Semester at Sea. It wasn't long, however, before two events shook the program and provided the ultimate test of commitment for its supporters.

On April 15, 1982, at the age of seventy-one, C. Y. Tung unexpectedly passed away in Hong Kong. The Tung family requested that part of his ashes be scattered at sea, on the Atlantic, Pacific, and Indian Oceans. His favorite ship, the SS *Universe*, was chosen to spread a portion of the ashes as it sailed home from its spring 1982 voyage. With the entire student body and faculty looking on in silence, the ship's master, Captain Yen, scattered the ashes in the Pacific Ocean. The *Universe* made three complete circles around the burial site before heading back on course for Seattle. With the man who made Semester at Sea financially possible now gone, the future seemed uncertain. Concerns about the program were put to rest by a letter from Mr. Tung's eldest son, Chee Haw Tung, to Dr. Max Brandt, the dean of the spring 1982 voyage. The letter said in part, "I do wish to take this opportunity of assuring

you and through you to your faculty members and the student body, that although my Father has passed away, his special dreams and project of the *Universe* will be carried on with vigor and with great efforts. I do hope as time goes by the program will achieve new heights." The Tung family was determined to carry on their father's work.

This determination could not have been more directly challenged than by the event that occurred as the *Universe* entered Alexandria harbor on the morning of February 25, 1983. It was a slightly overcast, windy day and the harbor seas were rough. The students on board were looking forward to their visit to the Middle East. A four-day stay was planned, but it turned out to be much longer. As the *Universe* slowly edged her way into the harbor mouth awaiting a pilot, she ran aground. There was only a slight jolt as the ship made contact with the mud and rocks of the ancient Egyptian harbor. There were no injuries among the passengers or crew. But as the *Universe* lay on the rocks well into the night, each hour brought further damage to her hull. Water filled her engine room, and her two boilers were substantially damaged. The following day harbor tugs pulled her free. However, soon after she was free the tow line separated and she began to drift. Through the courageous efforts of Chai Wing Chuen, the chief engineer, one boiler remained functional. The *Universe* limped into the harbor and was finally secured to the pier. Had she slipped outside the harbor, exposure to the rough seas might have brought an end to this precious vessel.

After the students were safely off the ship, Egyptian divers determined that the damage was extensive. The hull plates had separated, and damage extended through the double bottom of the vessel. The ship's emergency pumps were emptying 600 tons of water an hour out of the hull in order to keep the *Universe* afloat. Questions had to be answered that would affect not only the outcome of the spring 1983 voyage, but also the future of Semester at Sea. At this point the Tung family and the Seawise Foundation took swift and decisive action to save the ship and the program. Large wooden wedges were driven into the hull separations of the *Universe* to slow the flow of water and to act as a form of bandaid repair. She was towed to Greece, placed in dry dock, and partially repaired. She then sailed on her own to Japan, where she was completely refurbished.

Although the spring 1983 voyage was terminated, the academic program went on as scheduled. Under the direction of Dean Lewan of the Institute for

Shipboard Education and Academic Dean Tobias Dunkelberger of the University of Pittsburgh, the entire faculty, staff, and student body was transported by bus from Cairo across the Sinai to Jerusalem. There, in the Diplomat Hotel, the University of Pittsburgh established a temporary campus. Conference rooms became classrooms, hotel rooms became dorm rooms, and Israel became a laboratory. For six weeks the students lived, studied, and made short excursions, using as their home base the hotel that became affectionately known as the SS *Diplomat*. Costs for the temporary campus were borne by the Seawise Foundation. The completion of final exams on April 11 marked the end of what undoubtedly was the most unusual semester in the annals of shipboard education. But it was a semester that demonstrated the strength and determination of those who now followed in the footsteps of James Lough, Bill Hughes, and C. Y. Tung.

There is no final chapter to the history of shipboard education. The repairs to the SS *Universe* made her stronger than ever, and she sailed on schedule from Seattle on September 14, 1983 on her twelfth consecutive Semester at Sea voyage. It is impossible to measure or even describe the effect of these voyages on individual students. But Michelle Le Baron, a student on the first Semester at Sea voyage in the spring of 1977, gives us a glimpse in this description of her semester at sea:

> For the individuals involved, the voyage has been so much more than the touching of four continents, six seas, and ten countries. It has, like a microscope, brought into sharp focus priorities and ideas, and broadened our awareness. The decks have been a backdrop for a personal voyage of self-discovery. Immediacy and intensity have marked human relationships formed with others as well as encounters we have faced within ourselves. It is in this personal sense that the meaning of the trip is translated into each individual's life.
>
> In returning to familiar faces and places, we carry with us new perspectives and resultant energy, injected like a current into our lives. An experience has been ours which cannot be measured in seconds or even light years—it has touched our lives with a mark that is timeless.

Twice a year the SS *Universe* takes approximately four hundred college students around the world. These voyages carry on the spirit and objectives of Dean James Edwin Lough and his original voyage on the *Ryndam* in 1926. Students are given the rare opportunity to learn about their world from the world itself.

One such voyage began not too long ago from the port of San Francisco. On a crisp, fall day, with some 500 students on board, the SS *Universe* made her way out into the bay and headed for the Orient. Among the hundreds of people waving goodbye from Pier 35 was an eighty-two year old retired travel agent. Constantine Raises had a smile on his face as the ship disappeared from view and the students began their own voyage of discovery.

The 18,000-ton, 564-foot SS Universe at anchor.

Semester at Sea Today

The SS *Universe* is the only ship sailing the oceans of the world as a fully-accredited, liberal arts university. The University of Pittsburgh and a non-profit educational corporation called the Institute for Shipboard Education are the sponsoring organizations. The SS *Universe* is a middle-aged cruise ship with the soul of an adolescent. Twice a year this converted cargo-liner provides a home for four hundred college students on an around-the-world academic voyage. The one hundred day cruise provides lasting friendships and a lifetime of memories. Fifty days are spent at sea, studying, playing volleyball, watching sunsets, discussing life, laughing and crying. Fifty days are spent in foreign ports, meeting people, inspecting monuments, exploring cities, villages, and rural countrysides.

Students from universities and colleges throughout the United States participate in this unusual program. They receive University of Pittsburgh academic credit for their Semester at Sea. To qualify, students must have completed at least one year of college and be in good academic standing. The faculty for each academic voyage is selected from hundreds of applicants. Most faculty members have Ph.D. degrees and are selected not only for their teaching expertise, but also for their international experience. The shipboard academic program consists of lectures, readings, discussions, and field practica designed for each port of call. Classroom work and field experience combine to integrate the academic program with world exploration. A specially designed Core Course is required of all students and presents current social, political, and economic issues relating to each country visited. Core provides the background to the regions visited in order to make in-port experiences more meaningful. Outstanding regional experts frequently join the ship to address the Core Course as guest lecturers. The ship has a 10,000 volume library as well as a closed-circuit television system with a collection of hundreds of educational video tapes and movies. Sixty to seventy courses are offered each semester ranging from comparative economics and world politics to world art and modern theater.

The SS *Universe* is the dormitory, the lecture hall, the gymnasium, the faculty club, and the dining room for this floating campus. Students, faculty, and staff share living, dining and recreational facilities. There are fourteen classrooms, a theater, a large student union, a book store, and a hospital. Exercise bicycles, jogging track, volleyball/basketball court, swimming pool, and weight room make daily exercise possible.

Each trip begins and ends in the United States. Between the two ports of Miami and Seattle lies an itinerary of cities which may include Cadiz, Piraeus, Istanbul, Alexandria, Bombay, Hong Kong, Keelung, and Kobe. Twenty-five professors make the cruise an intense academic experience; twenty staff members make the trip an intense living experience; one hundred-fifty Chinese crewmen make the voyage a relaxed and comfortable one; and four hundred college students make it fun for all.

As students, faculty and staff board the ship, confusion reigns. The ship seems strange and congested; the new passengers feel displaced, apart from one another. As the days flow by, the ship becomes a sanctuary. When the ship and her participants approach the shores of the United States at the end of the voyage, they have become a close, caring community. They have learned to love their ship, and they have learned to respect, often admire, one another. They have also experienced the world.

The Departure

The world is a book
and those who do not travel read only a page.

St. Augustine

Last-minute loading takes place when the students arrive at the ship with luggage ranging from surfboards and bicycles to maps and dictionaries. Overleaf: Excitement and celebration mingle with pensive ambivalence as the ship prepares to cast off.

Left: An uncertain smile and a wave goodbye. Above: Tugs nudge the Universe *from her Port Everglades berth at the start of an Atlantic crossing.*

The Sea

Seas but join the regions they divide.

Alexander Pope

One of the many delights of participation in a Semester at Sea voyage is the closeness one feels with nature. From the surprise visits of sea mammals to the constantly changing interplay of sun and water, each day is enhanced by a heightened awareness of its unique beauty.

Above: The Universe *plows through an Atlantic typhoon. Right: Midway between Kenya and Bombay, India the pristine waters of the Indian Ocean surround the archipelago known as the Seychelle Islands.*

The Land

We have not inherited the earth from our fathers,
we are borrowing it from our children.

Lester Brown

Above: Located on Taiwan's north coast, Yehliu National Park is noted for its rock formations. Right: A communal rice field near Guangzhou, China.

Far left: A fragrant tea plantation in the Sri Lankan highlands.

Left and above: Rice is well suited to Sri Lanka's moist equatorial climate.

Left: Wearing plastic ponchos over their saris, Sri Lankan women work rice paddies in the rain near the hill country city of Kandy. Above: A field laborer inspects his newly planted rice in Sri Lanka. Right: Drawing well water in the south Indian state of Tamil Nadu.

Left: A Bantu village in the Transkei. Above: A Xhosa woman returning home with a load of firewood.

The Amboseli Game Reserve is located in southern Kenya near the Tanzanian border. With Africa's highest peak, Mt. Kilimanjaro, serving as a backdrop, this reserve is perhaps the most scenic on the entire continent. Gazelles, lions, cheetahs, and elephants are among the thousands of animals that roam the plains of Amboseli.

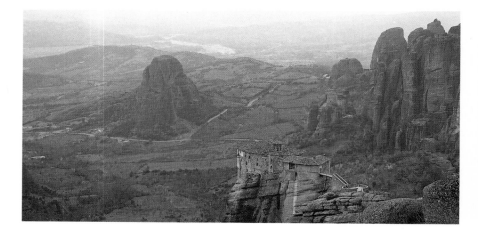

Above: The monasteries of the Meteora are built on the 1800-foot rock spire summits that tower above the northern Greek city of Kalabaka. Right: In southern Spain a sheepherder tends his flock at sunset in the hills above Granada.

The People of the World

Man himself is the crowning wonder of creation,
the study of his nature the noblest study the world affords.

William Gladstone

Left: Japanese school children. Above: A Buddhist temple in Kyoto.

Left: A student of Peking Opera at the Foo Hsing Opera School in Taipei, Taiwan. Above: A grandfather and grand-daughter in Shanghai, China.

Left: Guangzhou's best known and largest park, Yue Xiu, attracts Chinese as well as foreign visitors. Above: A four-year-old charmer salutes and smiles in Beijing. Right: A Beijing husband and wife. Overleaf: A policeman directs traffic in front of Tian An Men Square in the center of Beijing.

A calligraphy student practices his craft in Shanghai.

Facial massage is often part of the tai chi practiced in China.

Above: A Chinese child enjoys an apple on the streets of Beijing. Right: A Chinese woman takes a midafternoon rice and tea break in Guilin. Far right: A mother in Guangzhou displays a gift from a Semester at Sea student.

Above: A crowded outdoor market next to one of the thousands of small Hindu temples on the Indonesian island of Bali. Right: Women from the southern Indian city of Mahabalipuram carry their wares to market. The carved rock shrine seen in the background is the eighth-century Hindu Jalasayana or Shore Temple.

Far left: In order to attract attention, a young girl's face is painted, her tongue skewered, and her body decorated. Sent into the streets of Tiruchirapalli by her parents to ask for coins, she is one of India's thousands of professional beggars. At the end of her working day, she removes the skewer as easily as a pierced earring. Left: In Madras, siblings play with a small gift from a SAS student. Above: A breakfast of beans on a street in Bombay.

Left: One of the many thousands of homeless people who live and sleep on the streets of Bombay. Right: The sun and age-etched faces of three Indian women. Far right: Two holy men representing different Hindu sects. One of the oldest living religions in the world, Hinduism is unique in that it has no single founder. It is composed of countless sects, innumerable gods, and has no well-defined ecclesiastical structure.

Left: A resident of the Bombay streets. Above: A father pleads for rupees to feed his child in Mysore. Far right: Hindu men from the sacred city of Kanchipuram.

Left: A woman from Victoria, the capital and main port of the Seychelle Islands. Above: A young boy rests in the tall grass of the Transkei after undergoing circumcision, his rite of passage into manhood. Right: Uniformed secondary school children return home after a day of classes. Overleaf: Five young Xhosas enjoy the late afternoon sun of the Transkei.

Far left: The Masai are a nomadic, pastoral people, relying on their cattle for their daily existence. With the grasslands around her village barren, this Masai mother packs her belongings and prepares to seek better grazing lands in southern Kenya. Top and left: A Masai woman and child from Kenya. Above: A young resident of Crossroads, a squatter camp in Capetown, South Africa.

Far left: In Egypt, whether for transportation, the irrigation of crops, or the cleaning of pots and pans, the Nile provides. Left and above: Time and the Saharan sun have left their imprint on the faces of these Egyptian men. Overleaf: American students bring a smile to the face of one of Giza's many camel jockeys who daily work the crowds at the Pyramids.

In Egypt's Bahariya Oasis an old woman wears the marks of southern Saharan beauty, a qatrah, or gold nose pendant, and a chin tattoo.

Jews from all over the world cross this stone plaza to pray at Jerusalem's Western (Wailing) Wall.

Left: Two Greek girls smile shyly as they look out their hillside window above the cobblestone streets of Hydra. Right: Looking like Little Lord Fauntleroy, this lavishly attired Greek child attends an Independence Day parade in Athens. Below: Residents of the central Aegean island of Ios.

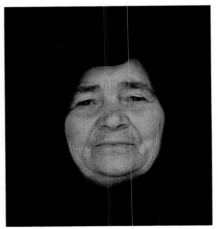

Left: A contemplative Turk in Istanbul. Right: Two lads from the Turkish city of Izmir on the Aegean Sea. Overleaf left: The colorful process of dyeing hides takes place daily at the tanneries in Fez, Morocco's artisan center. Overleaf right: Wearing a jellaba, Morocco's national dress, a man and his trusted companion bask in the morning sun of Marrakech.

Older women in Morocco still practice purdah, the traditional custom of Muslim women concealing their faces in public. Among middle-aged and younger women the practice is slowly disappearing.

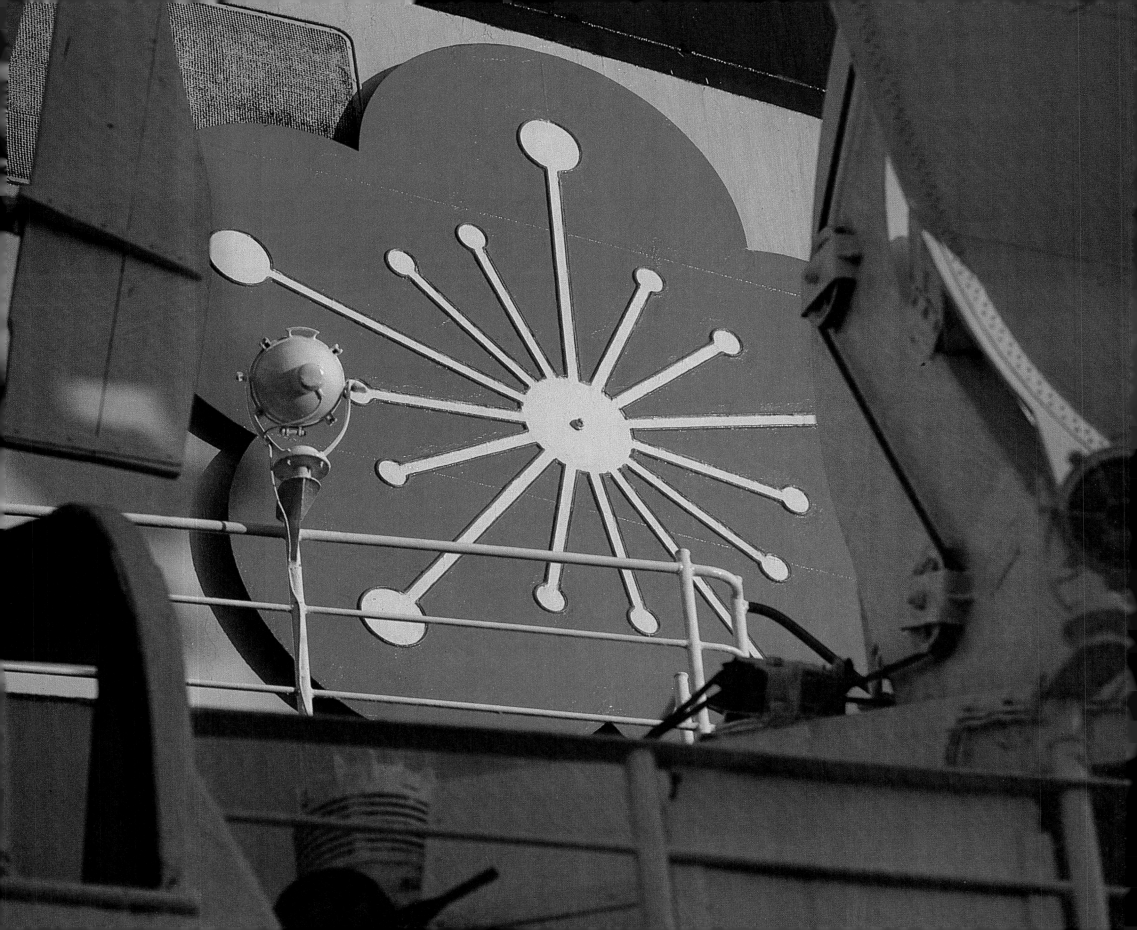

The SS Universe and Life at Sea

Traveling in the company of those we love

is home in motion.

Leigh Hunt

Left: The relaxed atmosphere of an outdoor class allows students to get a tan and an education at the same time. Right: Self-discipline is required to achieve a successful balance between work and play on board ship.

Although there is sufficient privacy for individual study, the closeness of the shipboard community provides an abundance of discussion opportunities. At right, a student receives a willing consultation from his economics professor, while others participate in an on-deck study group. Below: A professor scans the shelves of the ten-thousand-volume library.

Left: The Universe *is often met by representatives of local universities. Here Korean students from Busan University await the docking of the ship. Right: Students line the decks in anticipation of their arrival in Rio de Janeiro.*

Although few would consider ship-board food a gourmet's delight, it is more than adequate. For broccoli lovers, the cuisine is exceptional. Below left: A new, direct-dial cellular phone provides convenient access to friends and family at home. Below right: For those with barbering skills, three months at sea can produce significant supplemental income.

Left: Students often camp out on deck to enjoy the evening sea breeze and the glow of a sunrise at sea. Above: Students on trips that cross the equator participate in a special ceremony. King Neptune and Queen Minerva rise from the sea to preside over the trans- formation of these students from pollywogs into shellbacks.

The Chinese crew ensure the safety
and comfort of all on board. Above:
Two engineers enjoy a break from
the noise and heat of the boilers.
Right: A student and a ship's officer, Jing-Woei Jou, await the docking of the Universe. Jou has been
with the ship since its first
Semester at Sea sailing in 1977.

Despite the ship's small size in relation to an on-land campus, the Universe houses all of life's necessities, and many of its luxuries as well. Left: A game of volleyball takes place as the ship passes through the Suez Canal. Above: A jogger does his five miles up and down instead of around and around. Right: An animated game of water polo in the ship's saltwater pool.

Left: The morning and afternoon aerobics classes on the promenade deck are always well-attended. Right: A smaller but no less enthusiastic group attempts to imitate the Karate movements demonstrated by one of the crew. Overleaf: While her students explore the sights of Turkey, the Universe refuels and reprovisions in Istanbul.

The World as a Classroom

Seeing once is superior to hearing one hundred times.

Old Chinese Proverb

Left: A sitting Buddha near the entrance to the Ryoanji Temple in the western district of the city of Kyoto, one of Japan's ancient capitals. Above: The traditional "shoes off" during a lecture on Zen Buddhism in Kyoto.

Left: A colorful outdoor market in the port city of Keelung, Taiwan. Above: The Colonel is alive and well in the rebuilt city of Hiroshima, Japan. Right: The unusual cuisine of a popular restaurant in Pusan, Korea.

Left: A chinese junk passes in front of the modern skyscrapers of Victoria, Hong Kong Island's chief city. Right: Located in the south-western part of the island is the Aberdeen section of Hong Kong. Thousands live on board the junks and sampans that crowd the bay.

Millions of people in China use bicycles as their only means of transportation. At left is one of the many bicycle parking lots in Shanghai, China. Above: A SAS student makes a journal entry at Jaio Tong University in Shanghai. Right: Dawn at West Lake in the central China city of Hangzhou.

Left: China's Great Wall is the only human-made structure visible from the moon. Finished in the second century B.C., the wall is over three thousand miles long. Crumbling in many places, it has been restored at three mountain passes. This one, Ba Da Ling, is located about forty miles from Beijing. Right: At dawn, workers begin their ride to the factories of the industrial city of Guangzhou.

Ornate carvings are prominently displayed at religious shrines throughout the world. Left: The interior of a small Buddhist temple in Taroko Gorge, Taiwan is lit by the early morning sun. At right are small sections of the multicolored exteriors of the Hindu temples of Chidambaram in southern India.

*Above: A mighty rock fort over-
looks the city of Tiruchirapalli in
southern India. Right: Deeply af-
fected by the death of his beloved
wife Arjumand Banu in 1630, the
emperor Shahjahan built the white
marble Taj Majal as her memorial
and final resting place. It took the
finest craftsmen of Europe and
Asia twenty years to construct this
architectural wonder. The Taj is
located in Agra, about 125 miles
north of New Delhi.*

Left: A Hindu cremation ceremony in Agra, India. Above: An early morning bath in Chidambaram, India. Right: The Borobudur, the largest Buddhist temple in the world, is located near the central Indonesian city of Jogjakarta.

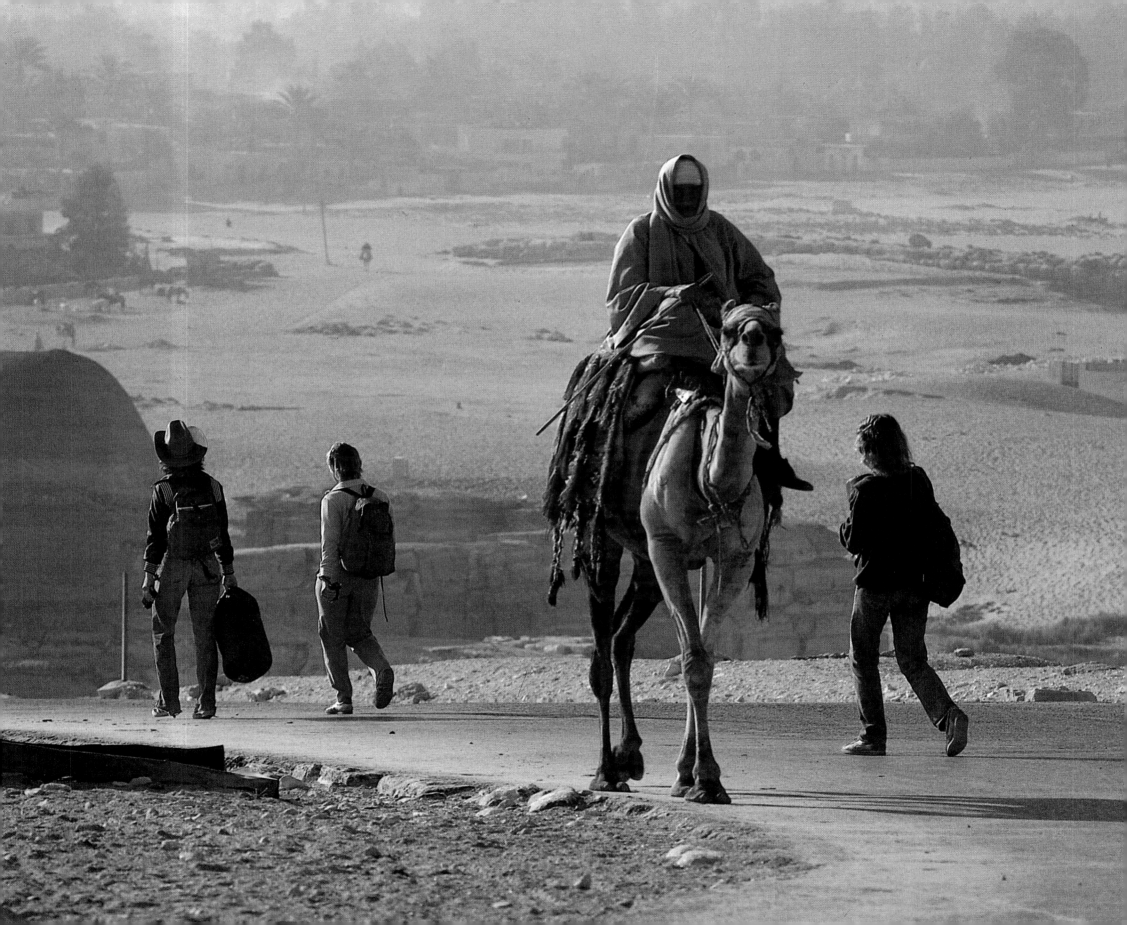

Two morning strolls in Giza—one along the paved roadway to the Sphinx and one across the desert toward the pyramids.

Left: Cheops, the largest of the Great Pyramids, stands 482 feet high with a base covering thirteen acres. According to Herodotus, this monument took a hundred thousand men twenty years to complete. Above: Egyptian sailing vessels called feluccas *provide transportation up and down the Nile. Right: The Great Sphinx of Giza was hewn from yellow limestone and dates back to 2620 B.C.*

Above: The Western Wall of the Old City of Jerusalem is the most sacred site of the Jewish religion. Right: Sitting atop Mt. Zion, just outside the wall surrounding the Old City, is the Church of the Dormition. It is believed that the Virgin Mary died here. Overleaf left: The Greek island of Ios is a popular destination for students. Whitewashed buildings are typical of the islands of the central Aegean. Overleaf right: The columns of the Temple of Poseidon rise from the Promontory of Cape Sunium about sixty miles south of Athens.

Left: The Doric columns of the temple of Athena rise from the crest of the Acropolis to dominate the surrounding city of Athens. Built under the supervision of the Greek sculptor Phidias in the fifth century B.C., the Parthenon served as a place of worship to the goddess Athena. With the decline of Athenian civilization, it became a Christian church and later a Turkish mosque. Right: A student relaxes on a hillside after a day of exploring the Aegean island of Ios.

Left: Workmen dyeing hides in the colorful if malodorous vats of a tannery in Fez. Above: The tower of Koutoubia Mosque in Marrakesh, Morocco.

The Experience

I am a part of all that I have met.

Alfred Lord Tennyson

Left: Faculty and students enjoy meeting the people of the world. Here, in the old Korean capital of Kyongju, a Semester at Sea professor and Korean school girls exchange "high fives." Right: A Semester at Sea student and Japanese high school girls exchange addresses near Nagoya.

Left: SAS students and Chinese children are the audience for a musical performance on the grounds of Zhongshen University in Guangzhou. Above: A generation apart in years, their homes separated by half a world, two ladies share a hug at a commune in Beijing, China.

East meets West again, above on the grounds of the Summer Palace in Beijing and at right with members of a Taiwanese marching band between parades in Taipei.

Left: Students from the University of Beijing and SAS compare notes in Beijing. Above: A member of the army of the Peoples Republic of China and a SAS student listen to a speech at Zhongshen University. Right: A SAS student joins a tai chi class in Guangzhou. Overleaf: Commercialism is evident in China as SAS students shop for souvenirs.

The gift of a Polaroid snapshot brings smiles to the faces of three Korean women in Pusan.

Pages 162–163: Students attend a presentation on Sri Lankan tea at a plantation near Nuwara Eliya. Left and right: SAS students share warm smiles and sincere words with a Bombay child and a Mahabalipuram woman. Above: A SAS student enjoys a midafternoon dip in the warm waters of the Bay of Bengal with a group of Indian students.

Above: A SAS student engages in a challenging discussion with an Egyptian man in Luxor. Right: Some horseplay on the plateau of the Transkei near its capital city, Umtata. Overleaf: Hundreds of camels are sold daily at auctions throughout Egypt. Here, in Cairo, a student gets an up-close and personal look at the merchandise.

Near Jerusalem and 1300 feet below sea level, students float in the 30 percent salt solution of the lowest lying body of water in the world, the Dead Sea.

The Final Port

The world is round and the place which may seem like the end
may also be only the beginning.

Ivy Baker Priest

OM & DAD,
URPRISE!!!
MOM & DAD,
THERE IS LIFE
BEYOND TEXAS!
HOOK EM'
PATTI AND JACK
I
LOVE YOU

America—the final port. Students return from their hundred-day voyage having seen and experienced the world. They have tasted it, touched it, smelled it, listened to it, watched it unfold with each new horizon. They have participated in an educational adventure unlike any other—A Semester at Sea.

Afterword

James Lough filed a $100,000 law suit against New York University, alleging that he had been wrongly discharged. The suit was settled out of court in 1931; Lough received $10,000 plus a small yearly stipend. After the war he continued to be involved in private travel/study programs, but never again attempted to organize a floating university. He died in 1953 at the age of eighty-one.

The old *Ryndam* never sailed again as a floating university. She was sold for scrap in Holland in 1929.

The MS *Seven Seas* was sold to the University of Rotterdam following her last voyage for the University of the Seven Seas. She was moored in Rotterdam and served until 1977 as a floating hotel for hundreds of the university's medical students. She was then sold for scrap in Belgium.

William Hughes stepped down as head of the Seven Seas Foundation in 1966. Despite failing health he continued to speak actively in support of shipboard education. He died in 1978 at the age of eighty-three.

The second *Ryndam* was bought by the Epirotiki Line. She was renamed the *Atlas*, and continues to make short, week-long excursions in the Mediterranean from her home port of Piraeus.

The cause of the fire on board the *Queen Elizabeth I* remains a mystery. She lay in the mud of Hong Kong harbor for close to two years before being blasted apart and removed piece by piece. Two of the *QEI*'s shore tenders were salvaged intact and placed on board the SS *Universe*.

The Seawise Foundation still exists. It provides the administrative vehicle through which the SS *Universe* is made available to the Semester at Sea program on a nonprofit basis. Headed by C. Y. Tung's two sons, Chee Hwa Tung of Hong Kong and Chee Chen Tung of New York, the foundation also offers scholarships to Chinese, Southeast Asian, and Latin American students for study on board the SS *Universe*.

C. Y. Tung's death was a great shock to his family and friends. His official funeral was held in Hong Kong. Thousands of people attended the Buddhist ceremony, which lasted for three days. Memorial services to commemorate his life were also held in New York and Taiwan. However, the most fitting and touching of all services in his honor were those conducted on board his ships. Three ships were used to scatter his ashes in the oceans of the world: the SS *Universe* in the Pacific, the *Canadian Explorer* in the Atlantic, and the *China Container* in the Indian Ocean.

Dr. John Tymitz serves as executive director of the Institute for Shipboard Education. Dr. Tymitz is responsible for all administrative and operational aspects of Semester at Sea.

Dr. M. A. Griffiths serves as the director of development for Semester at Sea, and heads the program's alumni office in Orange, California. He publishes "Shipmates," a quarterly newsletter that goes out to many of the twenty thousand alumni of all the shipboard education programs.

Dr. Lloyd Lewan, after twenty-one voyages around the world for World Campus Afloat and Semester at Sea, has left the program, but remains a consultant to the Institute.

Constantine Raises lives an active life in San Francisco. Considered the "dean emeritus" of California's travel agents, he lectures on world affairs and on his own travel experiences to senior citizens' groups. He keeps up a steady correspondence with over 200 old shipmates. He is eighty-five.

Bibliography

BOOKS

The Only Way To Cross, John Maxtone-Graham, the MacMillan Company, New York, New York, 1972.

The Atlantic Liners 1925–1970, Frederick Emmons, David & Charles: Newton Abbot, 1972.

C. Y. Tung: His Vision and Legacy. Michael Conners and Alice King, Seawise Foundation, 1984.

The Student Magellan, Yearbook for the 1926–1927 voyage of the Ryndam, Paul Robinson, Editor, 1927.

MASTERS THESES

The University of the Seven Seas: A Study of the Development of the University of the Seven Seas, Elizabeth Youngberg, Fresno State College, August, 1966.

The Origin and Development of Shipboard Education, Barry Marquardson, Arizona State University, May, 1981.

BROCHURES AND CATALOGS

"American University Tours," (under the auspices of New York University), Summer, 1923.

"The College Cruise Around the World—1926–1927," the University Travel Association.

"New York University Catalogue—1925–1926."

"The College Cruise Around the World—1928–1929," the University Travel Association.

"Floating University Bulletin," Volume II, Number 2, Address of President Sydney Greenbie, November, 1928.

"Third University Cruise Around the World—SS *Letitia*," University Travel Association, 1929.

"Floating University Catalog—1929–1930," International University Cruise, Inc.

"Traversity," Sydney Greenbie, 1931.

"A Year with the College Cruise versus a College Year Ashore—A Comparison," University Travel Association, undated.

"The Sixth Annual Floating University Cruise—1931–1932—SS *Resolute*," University Travel Association, 1931.

"The Seventh Annual Floating University Around the World Cruise—February 4–June 20, 1933—SS *President Johnson*," University Travel Association.

"University of the Seven Seas," Bulletin of the College Aboard the MS *Seven Seas*—1963–1964, University of the Seven Seas, March 1963.

"World Campus Afloat Handbook," Chapman College, undated.

"Odyssey II—The Ship Based Educational Concept," WCA Association, Chapman College, October, 1972.

"Chapman Today," Volume XXX No. 2, February, 1972.

ARTICLES

"Around the World," *Harper's Weekly*, September 1, 1877, pp. 689–690.

"The Good Ship Lollipop," Donald M. Murray, *Today's Education*, September–October 1976, pp. 33–37.

"SS *Universe:* Classrooms on the High Seas," Nicholas Rowan, *The Asia Magazine*, September 18, 1977, reprinted article.

"Around the World with the Floating University," Donald Davis, *The Rotarian*, June 1964, reprinted article.

MISCELLANEOUS

"A Brief History of the Floating Campus Concept," Dr. Ashleigh E. Brilliant, Chapman College WCA, June 1968.

"The Sea-Going School: How a Prayer for Peace came into Being," Dr. Gerald S. Black, a signed, undated statement.

"The Binnacle" Volume I, Number 1, September 17, 1926.

"Marco Polo Gazette," Volume One, Number 3, the Floating University, April, 1929.

"The Gangplank," an early Floating University Alumni Association Newsletter, Volume 3, May 1930.

Institute for Shipboard Education Newsletter, Volume 3, May 1977.

"Shipmates," Institute for Shipboard Education Alumni Newsletter, Number 13, Spring, 1982.

"History of USS Long Island," Navy Department, Naval History Division, Ships Histories Section, updated.

The documents cited in this bibliography and other supporting materiels were drawn from the following repositories:

University of Oregon, Library Special Collections Division, Eugene, Oregon.

University of Colorado, Western Historical Collections, Boulder, Colorado.

New York University, University Archives, N.Y., New York.

Semester at Sea Archives, Institute for Shipboard Education, Orange, California.

Phillip Sonnichsen private collection of shipboard education memorabelia and documentation, Los Angeles, California.

Designed and produced by James Stockton & Associates, San Francisco.
Composed by Typothetae and Omnicomp in Bodoni Book
with display lines in Bauer Bodoni.
Printed and bound in Singapore by Tien Wah.
Printing coordination by Interprint, San Francisco.

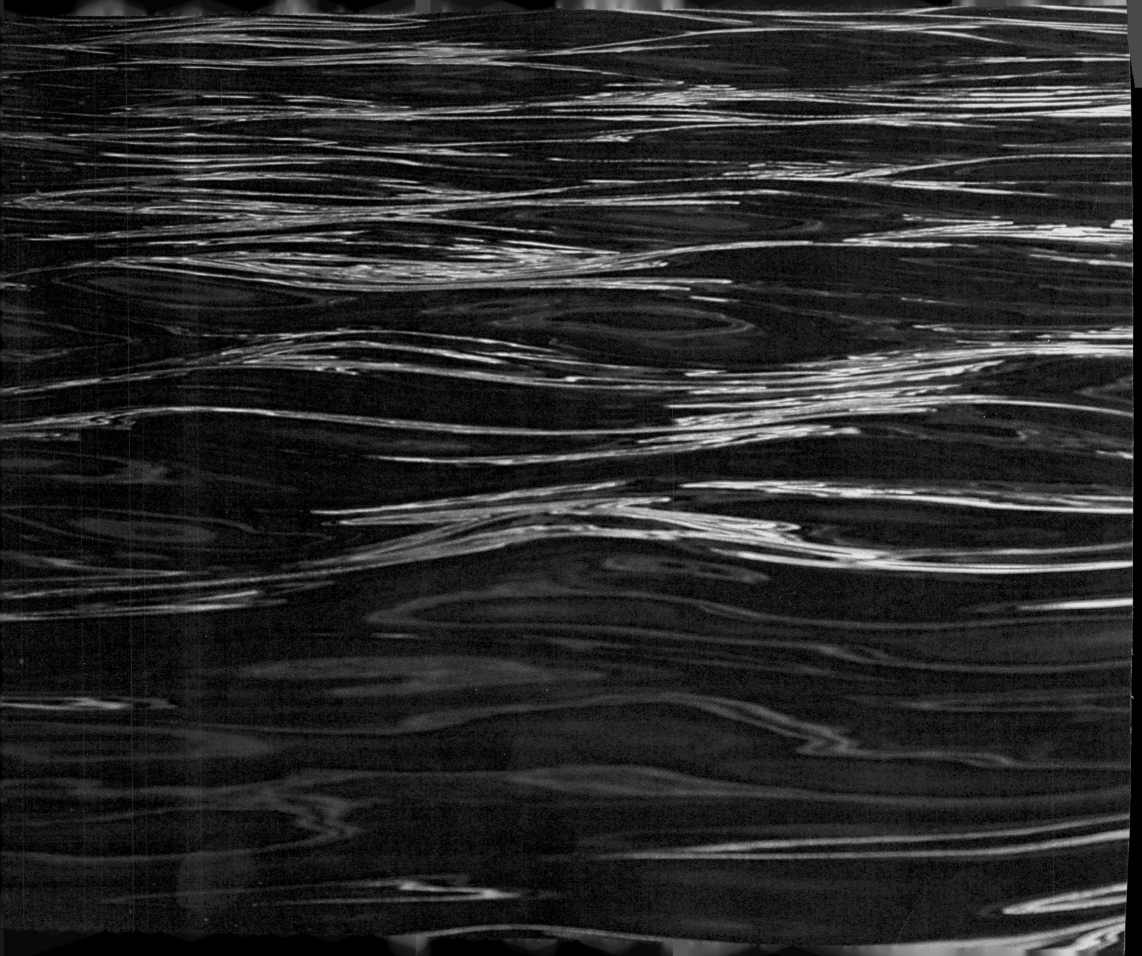